READ AWAY YOUR ACCENT

Is an accent making your spoken English difficult to understand?

Accents are charming, unless people can't figure out what you said.

"Read Away Your Accent" can help you improve your ability to be understood...the first time you say something!"

Written by

CHARLES MAGGIO & LAURA MAGGIO

A free audio version of the stories in this book is available online at

www.ReadAwayYourAccent.com

Use them to improve your spoken English!

Copyright 2019 Charles Maggio & Laura Maggio

ISBN: 978-1-7344867-0-4 (paperback)
       978-1-7344867-1-1 (ebook)

Cover and Interior formatting by TeaBerry Creative

CONTENTS

INTRODUCTION v

5 SHORT VOWEL SOUNDS

Furnishing an Apartment *Short /a/ sound as in apple* 1
The Bear "Attack" *Short /e/ sound as in elephant* 3
The Fish Prince *Short /i/ as in igloo* 7
A Doll for Polly *Short vowel /o/ sound as in octopus* 11
Monkey Trouble *Short vowel /u/ sound as in umbrella* 13

6 VOWEL SOUNDS

Nate's Interview *Long /A/ sound as in cake* 15
Christmas Eve in New York *Long vowel /E/ sound as in feet* 19
Ireland *Long /I/ sound as is pie* 21
A Boat That Floats...(well, sometimes!) *Long /O/ sound as in boat* 25
Future Universe *Long /U/ sound as in mule* 29
Out of the Blue *Long /oo/ sound as in flew* 33

18 CONSONANT SOUNDS

The Black Dog *Consonant /b/ sound as in bat* 37
A Cap for Good Luck *Consonant /k/ as in cat and kite* 39
Dining Out *Consonant /d/ sound as in dog* 43
The Fishing Trip *Consonant /f/ sound as in fan* 45
Beach Glass *Consonant /g/ sound as in glass* 49
Happiness *Consonant /h/ sound as in hat* 51
Joy *Consonant /j/ sound as in jam* 53
Animals, Animals, Animals *Consonant /l/ sound as in lip* 57
Summer Magic *Consonant /m/ sound as in map* 59
The Bird's Nest *Consonant /n/ sound as in nest* 61
Picking the Perfect Pet *Consonant /p/ sound as in pig* 63
The Surprise *Consonant /r/ sound as in rat* 65

18 CONSONANT SOUNDS

How to Use the New York City Subway System
Consonant /s/ sound as in sun..67
Tim's Tiny Turtle *Consonant /t/ sound as in top*....................................71
Avalon *Consonant /v/ sound as in van* 73
Winter Wonderland *Consonant /w/ sound as in wig*.............................75
Yes or No *Cononant /y/ sound as in yell*...79
Sunrise at the Zoo *Consonant /z/ sound as in zip*..................................81

7 DIAGRAPHS

Lucky Charm *Digraph /ch/ sound as in chin*...83
Sharks *Digraph /sh/ sound as in ship*..85
South to Portsmouth *Unvoiced /th/ sound as in thongs*......................87
Voiced /th/ sound as in feather 87
"Wh" Questions and More! *Digraph /hw/ sound as in whip* 89
Sing *Digraph /ng/ sound as in wing*..93
Trip to the Bank *Digraph /nk/ as in sink*...97

CONTROLLED VOWELS

The Circus Girl *Controlled vowel /ur/ as in bird & hurt*........................101
Going Far in a Car *Controlled vowel /ar/ as in park*............................105
The Short Storm *Controlled vowel /or/ as in fork* 109

3 DIPTHONGS

Boing, Boing, Boing *Dipthong /oi/ sound as in oil and boy* 113
Owl at Evening *Dipthong /ow/ sound as in ouch* 115
Learning to Cook *Dipthong /oo/ as in book and pull* 117

2 SPECIAL SOUNDS

Naughty Paul *Special sound /-aw/ as in jaw and haul*............................121
A Trip to Asia *Special sound /zh/ as in television* 125

INTRODUCTION

"Read Away Your Accent" was developed to help you reduce your accent, not to eliminate it. There is nothing wrong with speaking English with an accent, except when native English speakers cannot understand what you are saying.

"Read Away Your Accent" will help you master the 44 sounds of the English language. Each of the short stories focuses on one sound, which is indicated next to the story's title. While you should practice all of the sounds, some will be more challenging than others, depending on your native language.

Practicing with "Read Away Your Accent" enables you to practice in the privacy of your own space, without anyone listening. No need to feel embarrassed or self-conscious, as you practice the sounds of English. Also, learning to say the sounds while reading each text enables you to speak more fluently, rather than studying each sound in isolation.

The stories used in "Read Away Your Accent" were written in casual English, not academic English. These stories include many idiomatic expressions and colloquial American English phrases, which will help you speak more naturally and fluently. Over time, you will achieve more native-like, American-English speaking ability.

Unlike most books, "Read Away Your Accent" should be read over and over…not just one time. First read the stories one at a time silently. Then listen to the audio of that story, listening for the speaker's pronunciation, pauses, inflection, etc. Your goal should be to replicate the speaker's version, so that you can read along at the same time the speaker is reading. Your version should sound just like the speaker's. (It's a good idea to look up new words!)

NOTE: The font used for the stories in "Read Away Your Accent" is large, so that reading the stories many times will be easier on your eyes!

INTRODUCTION

SUGGESTIONS FOR USING THIS BOOK

This book is not only to be read once, but needs to be read over and over...and then read some more. A person who is truly committed to improving his/her pronunciation of the English language needs to spend a lot of time on each "sound story". Here is a suggested plan:

1. Read a sound story to yourself, silently. (Not out loud.)

2. Look up any words/expressions that are not familiar to you. (Google translate is a terrific tool!)

3. Listen to the audio version of the sound story, while silently reading the text. (Note: Pay particular attention to the pronunciation, pauses, intonation, inflection, and above all rhythm of the audio text. This is ESSENTIAL!)

4. Once you feel comfortable with all of the above, then read along with the audio text. This practice is known as "shadowing". At first, you may prefer to stop the audio after each sentence, or rewind the audio and listen again. As you are doing this in the privacy of your own space, there is no need to feel

self-conscious. By practicing this method, you will, over time, improve your ability to communicate more easily in English and be immediately understood!

Please don't despair! Reducing an accent takes time, determination, and WORK! If being clearly understood when you speak English is important to you, then "Read Away Your Accent" can be a very useful tool. There's no magic…just hard work.

After you feel comfortable with your ability to replicate the sound stories in "Read Away Your Accent", and all the 44 phonemes of English, you may want to try searching YouTube for songs with on-screen lyrics, and start to 'sing away your accent'!

Another method is to get an audio book of short stories with the accompanying text, and shadow each story as you previously learned to do with the stories in "Read Away Your Accent".

5 SHORT VOWEL SOUNDS

FURNISHING AN APARTMENT

Short /a/ sound as in apple

Congratulations! You have finally found the apartment of your dreams. Now you have to furnish and decorate your place to your liking. Apartments in large cities are usually small and expensive, but with some time and effort, you can make your place reflect your personal style and still stay within your budget. If your apartment comes furnished, then you can add your own individual touches to make it more personal in style. If your apartment is unfurnished, then you have some shopping to do!

Some things you will need to acquire will be furniture, lamps, kitchen items, bathroom accessories, dinnerware and flatware.

Sofas come in a large assortment of patterns, such as plaids, florals, and solid colors. Table lamps also come in many styles and sizes. Your shopping can be done in either high-end markets, department stores or in discount warehouses. Check for sales on needed items in newspapers and online, and also look for coupons to save you cash. Yard sales and garage sales may also surprise you with amazing treasures–who knows–you might just find that perfect salad bowl at a tag sale! A little dab of paint, an adorable cat lamp, and a cozy lap blanket may make your new apartment feel brand new. Most importantly, furnish your new pad with things that make you smile, laugh, and feel at home in your new abode!

5 SHORT VOWEL SOUNDS

THE BEAR "ATTACK"

Short /e/ sound as in elephant

Two of my friends and I planned to take a trip into the woods to go camping for a few days. We wanted to spend some time relaxing, before the school year began. We brought more than just the basic supplies, including a tent, bed rolls, mess kits, cellphones, flashlights, bread, eggs, cereal, power bars, etc. We thought we had planned it well enough and that things would go smoothly.

When we arrived at the campgrounds, we put my car into the parking lot and walked to the area designated for camping. It was going to be a camping trip, but not into the wilderness, as there would be facilities to make things less diffucult. Where we were headed, there was a medical station, restrooms, and a welcome desk, where they gave out information and maps of hiking trails. However, there was no store that sold food. The one surprise was the warning that we received about bears. They told us it was very important to be careful to not leave any food, or food garbage out, as there were brown bears living in these woods. We rolled our eyes thinking that they were being dramatic and overly cautious.

We proceeded to set up camp, and after about an hour of getting all set up, we had a sense of accomplishment, knowing that everything was taken care of. After the work of getting set up in the heat of the sun, we decided to use the map we were given, and to hike one of the nearby trails. It was a lovely, tree-lined path, not too steep, but not flat. Just perfect –enough of a challenge to make it interesting, but not an exhausting workout. When we returned from the hike a couple of hours later, we made a campfire, cooked up some hotdogs, ate, and decided to turn in.

In the middle of the night, outside of our tent we heard footsteps that we knew were not made by a person. These were definitely animal steps! We peered outside from the tent to see a bear walking about, looking for something to eat. We thought our provisions were kept far enough away from the tent, in what we thought was a 'safe' cooler. However, the bear was persistent, able to open the cooler, and helped himself to almost all of the food we had brought for the entire trip. Luckily, that was enough food to keep the bear happy, and we watched as he lumbered away from our tent area.

The next morning, not having much food left, we packed up all of our things and set off for home. While it was a short trip, it was cerainly an eye-opening one, and the next time we went camping, we knew enough to keep the food in the trunk of the car, even though it meant a long walk after eating. At least we never experienced another "bear attack" after that one time.

5 SHORT VOWEL SOUNDS
THE FISH PRINCE

Short /i/ as in igloo

Many children love to have bedtime stories read to them, and many of these stories are fairy tales about a prince and a princess. One of these is about the Fish Prince, which is an Indian folktale. The story goes like this…

Once upon a time there was a king and queen who had no children, which made the queen very sad. One day some fish were brought to the palace kitchen to be cooked for dinner, which was a very common occurrence. Among the fish was one unlike anything the cook had ever seen. Its scales sparkled with all the colors of the rainbow, and its head had a mark which looked like a golden crown. Just as the chef was about to cook the fish, the fish began to speak! The chef decided that this fish was too special to be cooked, so he put it in a small tank of water, thinking that this fish would make the queen very happy.

The queen was indeed very happy with the fish and she loved to watch it move quickly around the tank, showing off its beautiful colors. She became so in love with the fish that she named it "The Fish Prince", and called it her son.

As the fish grew bigger and bigger, he no longer fit in the small tank he was in, so the queen ordered that a huge tank be built for the Fish Prince to swim in. The queen would always carry some rice with her, and the fish would jump up from the tank to eat out of the queen's hand.

But one day the queen went to the tank and the beloved Fish Prince was not moving. His colors were very dull and he would not eat the rice that she brought for him. "Oh, my dear son, are you sick?" He answered, "I am not sick, but I am so lonely." The queen decided to have another very large tank built and had the workmen put it next to the Fish Prince's tank. Then she had her subjects look all over the kingdom for a girl to marry her son.

After a great amount of searching, they found the perfect girl, but she did not want to marry the big Fish Prince, because she was afraid of him. The girl decided to ask Father Cobra, a wise man/snake, for advice. Father Cobra was a seven-headed snake, who lived with his wife and his children near the bank of the river. Father Cobra told the girl, whose name was Balna, that the fish was not an ordinary fish, but was a handsome prince, who was being punished by the gods for having offended them. As punishment, he was turned into a fish. Father Cobra gave Balna three stones and told her to go into the tank next to the tank of the Fish Prince and during the night to throw one of the stones at the fish every time he went near her. After throwing the third stone, the spell was broken and the Fish Prince turned back into a handsome human prince.

The handsome human prince told her that she had saved both of their lives and now they could marry and live together as husband and wife. There was great rejoicing in the whole kingdom, and the Fish Prince, who was now a man prince, and Balna, the beautiful princess, were married and lived happily every after.

5 SHORT VOWEL SOUNDS

A DOLL FOR POLLY

Short vowel /o/ sound as in octopus

"Polly!" called Mom, "Get up now! We ought to get an early start for our shopping trip today." Eight year old Polly popped out of bed and got dressed quickly in her new orange frock. She gobbled down her corn flakes, popped on her scarf with the frog on it, and hopped into the car with her mom. This was a big shopping day for Polly–she was going to pick out a special new doll today.

Polly and Mom's first stop was a very large toy mart. They spotted the doll aisle and saw there were many to choose from. One doll was pretty, with long blond hair, twisted to look like an octopus. But it wasn't the exact type of doll Polly sought. So they left that store and headed to the mall. Once at the mall, they fought their way through the crowd to the top floor. There were two toy stores in the mall, but neither had the right doll for Polly. So onward they went again.

This time they drove into a nearby small town and found a little toy shop there. "Oh!" exclaimed Polly, "Look Mom, that's exactly what I want!" There on a top shelf was a doll that looked just like Polly, with soft locks of long blond hair and brown eyes. Polly loved the doll's frock covered with stars and her twinkly charm bracelet. "I'm so happy you spotted her", said Mom. They paid for the doll and headed to a diner for a quick meal, where Polly ordered her favorite coleslaw. Mom reminded Polly to keep the doll away from her baby brother, Tommy, as he might maul her! "What will you name your doll?" asked Mom? Polly thought for a moment and said, "Honestly, I would like to name her Swan, because she is so lovely." Mom smiled and they started home with their perfect purchase.

5 SHORT VOWEL SOUNDS

MONKEY TROUBLE

Short vowel /u/ sound as in umbrella

Spuds and Buddy were two rambunctious monkeys who lived in a zoo enclosure that resembled a beautiful jungle. Spuds was a full-grown adult and Buddy was a younger adult. Their keepers, Umberto and Ulrich, called them "double trouble" because they were always pulling crazy stunts on each other and on their keepers. For example, when Spuds was trying to sleep in the warm sunshine, Buddy would bust him with a dull thud of his hand, just to wake Spuds up. Spuds would wake up with a start and then bust Buddy back. Spuds would try to find a new sleeping spot in their little hut, just to be alone, but Buddy would always hunt him down and bother him. Thus, there was no rest for the weary Spuds!

One time, Spuds decided to get back at Buddy. Instead of filling his mug with water from the hose in their little jungle, Spuds lugged the hose near Buddy, spun around, and doused him with cold water. Buddy was stunned and tried to run, but ended up tripping over their bathtub, which was full of sudsy water. Buddy tried to get out of the sudsy tub, but ended up tipping it over, causing a big, soapy flood. Both monkeys just looked at each other and starting howling, because to them, this was very funny. As they began to rub soapy water all over each other, Umberto and Ulrich came by to see the unusual sight. Both agreed that Spuds and Buddy were two nuts and were definitely "double trouble"!

6 VOWEL SOUNDS

NATE'S INTERVIEW

Long /A/ sound as in cake

Nate, who is an ace tennis player, often loses track of time. Although a very good student at college, he sometimes gets so involved with what he is doing that he forgets everything else. His dad says jokingly, "Nate often gets lost in space!" No one is ever surprised when Nate shows up late. They just roll their eyes. Today, however, is different...he just cannot be late!

Nate will be graduating from college in a few months and he needs to make sure that he secures a space in the summer internship program at a local attorney's office. Nate plans to go to law school after college and the attorney in town allows future lawyers to work in his office during the summer breaks from school. He does put them through their paces, even though it is an unpaid position. It is a great way to help learn about how law really works, and if an intern does a good job, there is a chance that the law firm will give that person a job, once they have earned their law degree.

"Nate has been interested in law ever since he was a baby", his mother sometimes says. The truth is that for Nate, studying law never gets stale. He spends much of his free time reading about law, criminal trials, and articles about how the legal system works.

Therefore, today is very important for Nate to make a good impression on the attorney who will be interviewing him. Lately, he has been role-playing this interview in his mind, imagining the questions he will be asked, and what he will say in response. He wants this internship so much he could practically taste it!

Nate got ready, making sure to be on time. He got a haircut yesterday, put on his best suit, and spent much more time than usual in front of the mirror. His aim was to be sure he looked his best. On the drive to the interview, Nate was thinking about how the interview would go. He knew he would do his best to secure a place as an intern. As he got out of the car he thought to himself, "Well, I have prepared as much is I could, and now it's in the hands of fate!"

6 VOWEL SOUNDS

CHRISTMAS EVE IN NEW YORK

Long vowel /E/ sound as in feet

Most New Yorkers agree that it's a real treat to be in New York City on Christmas Eve. We are always eager to take a leisurely stroll to see the beautiful sights like the really huge tree in Rockefeller Center, the lovely wreaths on the doors and ceilings, the dreamy store windows and the shiny lights that seem to weave like radiant stars up and down the busy streets. The snowy sidewalks may tempt you to try to ski along the roads. It's nothing like sunny Phoenix would be in the winter!

People are in a merry mood, and seem eager to equally spread and receive both good cheer and feelings of peace. For recreation, you may be eager to seek out a neat show at Radio City Music Hall that guarantees to be another treat. During the Christmas season, these shows feature a holiday theme, complete with singing, dancing and a brief, but sweet, Nativity scene. Young and old will squeal with delight, as it is an unbelievable sight to see!

If a holiday shopping spree is something you need to achieve, there is no region superior to New York City. Depending on how much money you want to spend, you can find things that are really cheap, very dear, or roughly in between. Later you may feel like seeking out a convenient place to eat. Whether it be a fancy eatery for a lengthy feast or a speedy meal from a dealer on an intriguing street corner, there is always something to meet everyone's needs. After spending a delightful time in New York City on Christmas Eve, we guarantee you'll want to return again. It is the key to a wonderful holiday experience!

6 VOWEL SOUNDS

IRELAND

Long /I/ sound as is pie

Ireland is an island nation in the North Atlantic Ocean, separated from Great Britain by the North Channel, Irish Sea and St. George's Channel. Ireland is the third largest island in Europe.

The island's geography is made up of low-lying mountains, surrounding a central plain. Because of its mild climate, the country of Ireland has lush vegetation. The major crops grown in Ireland are wheat, oats and barley, all important grains. These are, of course, used in the making of Irish beer, which is famous world-wide. Many people love an ice cold beer when the weather is hot...perfect! Especially an Irish beer in Dublin! Apples, strawberries, blackberries, gooseberries, loganberries and raspberries are also grown in Ireland. These can all be used to make great pies, which are another specialty from Ireland.

Dublin, which is Ireland's capital city, has many ideal things to see and do. The Liffey River runs right through the city and has many walkable bridges for people to cross. These bridges might remind some people of Paris. There are, of course, too many sights to name them all, but there is a must-see spot in Dublin known as Trinity College.

Founded in 1592 by Queen Elizabeth I, Trinity College is a lovely place of peace and beauty. It is Ireland's oldest educational institution and is the best in terms of rankings. Actually, there was an older university, built in 1311, which was called The Medieval University of Dublin, but it ran out of funds and disappeared during the Protestant Reformation.

Trinity College boasts famous alumni, such as Oscar Wilde and Samuel Beckett, who were both literary personalities. Several well-known political figures such as Theobald WolfeTone, Henry Grattan and President Mary Robinson were also Trinity graduates.

6 VOWEL SOUNDS

There is a funny story about Trinity College, which has to do with a superstition and involves the campanile (bell tower). The bell tower was added in 1853 and stands over 100 feet tall. Tourists love to see the tower, but students are very cautious due to a superstition which says that any student who is unfortunate enough to pass underneath the bell tower while the bell is tolling, will fail their college exams. So students make sure not to walk underneath the campanile!

Trinity College was not always in the city center as it is today, but it was once located outside and to the east of the walled city of Dublin. The campus is a mix of classical and contemporary buildings, and Sunday morning is the best time to visit. On Sunday morning you can walk around with few crowds to detract from the beauty of the college. Include a visit to Ireland in your future travel plans!

6 VOWEL SOUNDS

A BOAT THAT FLOATS... (WELL, SOMETIMES!)

Long /O/ sound as in boat

Years ago, when I was in high school, my goal was to own a boat. Boats, I thought, we're cool to have, great fun during the New York summers and good transportation, too! That is, of course, if the boat would float!

New boats were very expensive, so I decided to buy a used boat. While new boats are pristine and beautiful, a fresh coat of paint could make a used boat look like a show piece! After a lot of searching for the perfect boat, I found a 17 foot fishing boat in white and turquoise, which I thought would look great! The outboard motor was only 50 horse power, but I wasn't planning on boat racing, so that didn't matter, A friend who knew a lot about boats came with me, and agreed that this would be a fine boat to own. After buying the boat, motor and trailer, we brought it back to my house to show my family. Everyone jumped for joy at the promise of spending the summer on the Great South Bay of Long Island.

I spent the next few weeks working on the boat, getting it ready for its "maiden voyage". It had a fresh coat of paint, newly upholstered turquoise seat covers, and the newly refinished natural wood deck shone like a new copper penny. The boat was therefore named "Penny" and was all set to go.

My friends and I trailered the boat to the south shore of Long Island, in order to launch it from Bay Shore, which is a town on the Great South Bay directly across from Fire Island. Shortly after we put the boat in the water, it sprang an unexpected (and unwanted!) leak and began to slowly take on water. We quickly started to bail out the water and got the boat back to shore, re-trailered it, and brought it back to my garage. We found the small hole, patched it securely, and soon it was ready to be launched again.

Thankfully, that was the last problem we had with the boat and we used it during the remaining two summers of high school. After that, I started college and worked part-time, so I no longer had that much free time, even in the summers. I sold the boat. It was fun while it lasted and I have great memories of the boat that at first wouldn't float. "Penny" made for a lot of fun times on the Great South Bay those two summers!

6 VOWEL SOUNDS
FUTURE UNIVERSE
Long /U/ sound as in mule

For almost as long as people have been on earth, many have wondered about how things would be in the future universe. There are many authors who have written about the future and out of this came the genre of books/stories/films known as science fiction, commonly called sci-fi. The Brave New World, Starship Troopers and Dune are just a few examples.

During the two years, 1964-1965, New York City hosted the World's Fair, the theme of which was "The World of Tomorrow", or what life would be like in the year 2000. The World's Fair was part theme park, part museum. It posed the question, "What new inventions would be available to humans who were to live in the future?" They predicted flying cars, humans living in outer space and telephones that would enable you to see the person you were talking to. Of course, some of these predictions came true, but many are still years away.

The symbol of the 1964-65 World's Fair was a giant stainless steel globe, showing all seven continents. The globe named "The Unisphere" still stands on the original site in Flushing Meadows –Corona Park, where the World's Fair was held. You should Google the Unisphere to see a picture of this beautiful steel sculpture, built to represent "Peace Through Understanding", the motto of the Word's Fair. It is known as the symbol of a peaceful and happy tomorrow.

Many people today still ponder the future. Will there be cures for many of the diseases that exist today? How will humans live and what will their homes look like? Will humans take rockets to other planets the way that we take planes to other countries?

Surely no one knows for sure what the future will bring. We have come a long way from the days when people thought the earth was shaped like a cube and not the sphere as we know it to be. Today we can go to sleep in New York City and wake up in Asia, Will that be true of travel to distant planets in the future? Although no one is sure about what the future will bring, it is fun thinking about what will happen many years from now. It's interesting to think about the future of the universe and the impact on human beings and the planet Earth!

6 VOWEL SOUNDS

OUT OF THE BLUE

Long /oo/ sound as in flew

My friend, Sue, an ESL teacher was planning a trip to Hawaii to celebrate her birthday. Her friend, Suzanne, was going, too. They were both excited about the trip, especially Sue, who would actually turn 30 on the big Island of Hawaii. As the school year was ending in two days, Sue and Suzanne planned to fly to Hawaii as soon as the school year ended.

As planned, Sue and Suzanne arrived in Hawaii and were surprised when the agent who met them said there was a three-mast sloop waiting to take them to their hotel, which was on a tiny island off of the big island. The trip was already turning into an adventure, as they had never been on that type of boat before. Shortly after they arrived at their hotel, they changed into their bathing suits, and we're soon lying near the hotel's luxurious pool. This trip was already showing signs of being a great adventure.

Sue was hoping to spend her 30th birthday relaxing, as the school year had been pretty hectic. Truthfully, she was having difficulty with the thought of no longer being in her 20's! She felt she wasn't yet ready to start the process of "adulting". Suzanne was great about encouraging Sue whenever she noticed Sue looking sad or sullen. Suzanne was terrific about lightening the mood, However, the best was yet to come!

After swimming in the pool, getting dressed and having a relaxing dinner in the hotel, the two friends decided to go to sleep early, as the trip, plus wine with dinner, was pretty tiring and they were both pooped. The following day was Sue's actual birthday, so she wanted to be refreshed for that, even though she knew nothing special was planned. They both fell asleep as soon as their heads hit the pillows.

6 VOWEL SOUNDS

The girls planned to take the sloop back to the big Island and to do some shopping in the Kona area, which is famous for its amazing shops that everyone said just blew them away! They heard there were fantastic clothing shops, stores that sold things made from Koa wood, which is beautiful wood found only in Hawaii. They knew the name of a good waterfront restaurant someone had recommended and planned to have lunch there. So, after some successful shopping, they headed to the restaurant. Once there they asked for a table facing the water.

Out of the blue, and right on cue, six of Sue's and Suzanne's school colleagues appeared at the table the waiter escorted them to. Sue was genuinely surprised, but Suzanne was, of course, the one who did the planning. Once Sue knew what was going on, she couldn't believe how well Suzanne hid the surprise from her. That wasn't the end of the surprises, though. There were tours, shows and all kinds of adventures planned for the birthday girl. This was not going to be the relaxing vacation Sue had thought about, but was even better, as it took her mind off turning 30.

18 CONSONANT SOUNDS

THE BLACK DOG

Consonant /b/ sound as in bat

The blaring blast of the booming bell signaled the end of the school day for Brandon and his two best friends, Bart and Bobby. The boys bolted out into the bright spring sunshine and began the brief walk home. They were neighbors and lived very close by to each other. As they were walking and talking boisterously, Brandon thought he heard a bizarre little sound in the blue hydrangea bushes that were just beyond the schoolyard. "Listen", he said to his buddies, "Do you hear something in the shrubbery?" Both of the other boys came to an abrupt stop and listened as well. "There's some kind of sobbing sound coming from beyond there", said Bart. "Let's observe what's making that bleating noise!" agreed Bobby. The boys carefully parted the branches and discovered what was making the bothersome hubbub. It was a beautiful Black Lab puppy!

"I think he's stuck", said Brandon. "Let's help him break free and establish that he's all right." They liberated the bawling baby dog and carried him briskly to Brandon's nearby home. Brandon showed the Black Lab puppy to his parents, who corroborated that he was just scared, and not bruised or broken. "Can we keep him? Please, Please!" begged Brandon. Brandon's parents put an ad in the neighborhood paper and signs around several blocks, but nobody claimed the puppy. "I guess he's our beautiful bouncing boy now", said Brandon's father. "What should we name him? We can't keep calling him 'Black Dog'!" Brandon had given the puppy's name considerable thought and bellowed, "Dad, his name should be Bo, after your favorite musician, Bo Diddley. Do you believe you like that name?" Brandon's dad bobbed his head and said, "I absolutely approve!" Brandon and Bo stumbled happily outside to broadcast the fabulous news to Bart and Bobby. Bo now belonged to Brandon and was the best dog ever!

18 CONSONANT SOUNDS

A CAP FOR GOOD LUCK

Consonant /k/ as in cat and kite

Back in college, my best friend Kenny liked to play baseball and joined the men's baseball team. He was actually a very good baseball player and was the catcher for the team. His father Carl, had also been a baseball player, and had made it to the minor leagues when he was Kenny's age. Like many baseball players, Kenny wore a baseball cap that he insisted was the reason they won so many games. It was his lucky cap, he'd always say.

As time went by, Kenny, doing better and better for the team, figured that the cap was not just lucky for baseball. He started to wear the cap everywhere he went. After awhile, people started teasing him about it, asking if he was going bald, and was the cap a cover for his "secret"? It wasn't though, as Kenny had a full crop of hair. He just believed that the cap was his lucky charm.

One day, some of Kenny's friends asked us if we wanted to go out on their motor boat in the big river behind the college. We said, "Sure!", and soon we were off cruising the river. It started out a beautiful day, but an unforecasted storm was approaching and the wind really picked up. All of a sudden, a very powerful wind gust blew by and snapped Kenny's cap right off his head. Try as hard as we did, we couldn't catch the cap and it was soon gone, carried by the powerful winds. Kenny thought he was going to be sick. He couldn't believe that his lucky cap was lost forever.

No one spoke as we made our way back to campus, but everyone was thinking the same thing –about Kenny's cap. When we arrived back at the starting point where we had left the car, everyone just parted with a very quick "goodbye". None of the usual teasing and silly jokes. No one felt like talking. Three days later the baseball championship game would be played and everyone 'wondered, was the cap really the cause of Kenny's good luck? Time would tell.

18 CONSONANT SOUNDS

On the day of the game, we all thought that Kenny would be wearing a new cap to replace "ol' lucky", as Kenny fondly referred to his "now missing" cap. However, that was not the case. Many people didn't recognize Kenny at first, until he took his catcher's position. The head of hair they had forgotten he had was the reason. The game was close, but Kenny's team did win and and Kenny felt very relieved. He finally had to admit that it was his skills that helped win the game, and not the cap that he thought brought good luck.

He did, however, buy a new cap!

18 CONSONANT SOUNDS

DINING OUT

Consonant /d/ sound as in dog

Dining out is one of the most delightful things to do. Whether it be with Mom and Dad, sisters or brothers, a date or with dear friends, dining out provides not only a break from cooking at home, but also a time to try new types of foods, if you dare!

Cities offer the largest selection of diverse types of foods that you can try, though suburban and rural areas now do as well. Italian restaurants offer delicious types of pasta, and a wide variety of fish and meat dishes, too. Add a chilled bottle of wine and your meal will be even more delightful. Dining at a French restaurant will persuade you to try rich, dense sauces that add amazing, decadent flavor to any dish. Asian cuisine delivers distinct flavors to their food through the use of tasty spices and seasonings that deliver rich boldness to their dishes. Try some delectable noodle soup with seafood and mixed vegetables, and your stomach will be filled with warm, amazing goodness!

Casual dining is also available in almost all destinations. Fast-food restaurants are found in practically every town you find. You can grab a quick hamburger and fries, hotdogs, pizza and many other goodies practically anywhere. Many fast-food places even provide special smaller meals for kids, which they find just "delish"! It's important to watch your food choices though, and make sure you eat a balanced diet that suits your body's needs and keeps you healthy. With all the different types of foods available, it should be easy to make good food choices, while still having delectable dishes that keep your tummy filled!

18 CONSONANT SOUNDS

THE FISHING TRIP

Consonant /f/ sound as in fan

One fine Friday summer afternoon, Fiona's father Joseph decided to take the family fishing. "Go find your sister, Franny", said Father, "The weather is so delightful that we don't want to waste the afternoon." Fiona asked Father if her cousin Christopher could come along as well. "Call him on the telephone and make sure his parents say he can come with us -we don't want him to miss out on the fun." Christopher had permission to join Fiona's family and helped them fill Father's fire engine red Ford Fiesta with all the fishing gear.

After a short drive, they finally arrived at their favorite dock, which they frequented often. The dock was near a sandy cliff covered with scruffy pine trees. The children helped Father lift all the fishing gear out of the Ford and loaded it into the small skiff Father had rented for the afternoon. Father helped Fiona, Franny and Christopher bait their hooks, using his fishing knife to cut each one half a worm to feed to the fish. Franny wanted a whole worm, but Father felt that half a worm was enough. Before Father could bait all the hooks, Fiona felt a tug on her line and quickly pulled up a flopping, fat flounder. Shortly after, Christopher had a fish on his line, and then Franny followed. Father could barely keep up with all the baiting and fish removal! Before long they had a bucketful of flounder. With all the fun they were having, no one noticed the rainfall starting to pound down on them, and that the flow of the water had caused them to drift further out to sea. Father told the children they had to head for shore, but the kids wanted to finish their fishing day. Finally they fled back to shore, returned the skiff, and got back into the Ford to head for home. Soaking wet but fabulously happy, the three children and Father were met at the door by Franny's and Fiona's mother, Phyllis. Standing with her arms crossed and frowning, she furrowed her eyebrows and furiously growled at Father, "Joseph, I was so fearful! It's pouring outside! You were gone for a frightfully long time! Why didn't you notify me to let me know you were safe?!" Father felt his pocket and realized he had forgotten to bring his cell phone. "Forgive me, dear Phyllis! We didn't mean to frighten you! Next time I promise not to forget my phone. Did you see all the fine flounder we caught today?" With that, Phyllis laughed and said, "You are all forgiven. I'm looking forward to a wonderful fish fry feast tonight!"

18 CONSONANT SOUNDS

BEACH GLASS

Consonant /g/ sound as in glass

Walking along the graceful curve of a beach shoreline can garner many advantages. The gentle lapping of the waves generates a calming, relaxing mood and helps alleviate damaging stress. Looking out at the green or blue water gives the mind a break from the ongoing grind of everyday life. But don't just glance at the water, gaze down at the ground as well, for there are generous treasures to be gathered there. Gorgeous seashells, strange rocks and glistening beach glass can be gathered on most any beach.

Beach, or sea, glass is a popular thing sought out by eager collectors. It is most generally found in areas that brag a rich history, or where age-old galleons were submerged ages ago. Broken shards of glass are tumbled by gentle or gigantic waves, softening their edges and giving the glass a smooth glow. Beach glass comes in a huge hodgepodge of colors, more than you could ever guess. They range from the common grass greens, ghostly egg whites and ginger browns to the rare outrageous oranges, regal reds and golden yellows that are tough to find. There are many strategies for rummaging for beach glass, one of which is the methodology of zigzagging back and forth across the ground. Rocky, pebbly beaches often garner the most glass, as the small pieces can get caught amongst the stones or under gnarled, gnawed logs of driftwood. The glint of the glass in the sun will be a sign that it is indeed glass, and not a stone or rock. Bring a bag for the storage of your treasures, sunglasses to block the sun's glare, and good walking shoes to guard against fatigue. Gaze down at the ground and make a game of challenging yourself to gain new pieces each time you go gathering. Beach glass collectors can never seem to get enough! You may want to catalogue your findings in a log as well. No one can argue about the intrigue of snagging such colorful treasures that man and nature have so generously scattered for sea glass gatherers to conglomerate and delight in.

18 CONSONANT SOUNDS
HAPPINESS

Consonant /h/sound as in hat

Hannah and Harvey were meeting their best friends Hilary and Howie for dinner that night at one of their favorite teahouses in Harlem. Both couples had agreed to meet at six o'clock and wanted to de-stress after having had harrowing days at work. As they entered the teahouse, the handsome host with the highlighted blond hair asked them whose name the reservation was under. Hannah said it was under hers, and they were seated posthaste. "It's so good to finally sit down and relax", said Howie, "Work has just been so hard on me lately." Hannah, Harvey and Hilary all heartily agreed. "Instead of rehashing all of our work headaches and heartaches, let's all come up with one thing that makes us feel truly happy", suggested Hilary. "That's hunky-dory!"

hollered Howie. "Who wants to go first?" Hilary said she would start, as it was her idea.

"Happiness to me is a walk along the beach, enjoying the hazy sunshine and hoping to find some sea glass", said Hilary. "All my apprehension about my job just seems to disappear." Hannah offered to go next and said, "For me, I am most happy holding the hand of my wonderful husband Harvey and just snuggling on the couch in our house." "Ha-ha!" said Harvey, "I heartily agree, just add in a heaping bowl of hot wings and that's what makes me truly happy!" Everyone had a good laugh and then turned to Howie for his definition of happiness. "What makes me honestly happy is just what we have right here, right now– hanging out with my beautiful wife and wonderful friends fills my heart with happiness and makes all the harassment at work seem less heavy." "Here's to being happy!" The four friends all heartily agreed.

18 CONSONANT SOUNDS

JOY

Consonant /j/ sound as in jam

Joy: jubilation, great pleasure, joyfulness, enjoyment, happiness, joie de vivre.

- Joy can be found in simple things or in majestic happenings.

- Joy can be the first dandelion emerging in the lawn after a long, frigid winter.

- Joy is watching the jays and juncos jockeying and jumping for position at the edge of the birdbath for a drink.

- Joy is welcoming home a soldier with a badge for courage.

- Joy is rejoicing in becoming a parent when you had just about given up.

- Joy is receiving that gigantic package in the mail from your first–choice college.

- Joy is waking to the exaggerated song of a sparrow on a July morning.

- Joy is doing what you love and earning wages as well–the perfect job!

- Joy is warm toast spread with juicy strawberry jam or jelly.

- Joy is a jaunty walk on the beach with a pocketful of jingle shells and an undamaged piece of jade–colored sea glass as well.

- Joy is feeling the large, slimy tongue of a huge ginger giraffe as you feed him cabbage in his cage.

18 CONSONANT SOUNDS

- Can a fly feel joy after being trapped behind a window and then is finally freed to the outside by a gentle hand?

- Joy is finding contentment and enjoyment at any age.

- Joy is always tangible for you, if you just let it into your life.

18 CONSONANT SOUNDS

ANIMALS, ANIMALS, ANIMALS

Consonant /l/ sound as in lip

Our beautiful Earth is full of millions of species of animals, living in multiple, diverse locations. Oceans, jungles, woodlands, and even backyards are loaded with countless varieties of wildlife. Look at your lawn carefully and you will locate ladybugs, long caterpillars, and green leafcutter ants concealed in the grass. Walk for a spell through a lovely forest and listen carefully to the delightful calls of meadow larks and cardinals. If you fill your hand with sunflower seeds and stand quietly in the woods, little black-capped chickadees may alight and feed right from your palm. It is quite a marvelous experience!

Our oceans are also full of millions of various types of animals that live in the water. From the colossal blue whale to the miniscule little goldfish, the seas are teeming with underwater life that is spectacular to behold. Lionfish, eels, walruses, sea lions, corals, jellyfish, sea turtles, salmon, clams, lobsters and mussels are just a few of the many sea animals you might glimpse when you explore the ocean.

Jungles are full of many types of animals as well. In Africa, lions patrol the grasslands, looking for prey and sleeping with their little cubs. Lanky giraffes pluck tasty leaves from lofty treetops. Graceful gazelles leap across the grasslands, avoiding the lions and leopards who are often trailing them. Hulking elephants lumber across trails, looking for the nearest water hole for a cooling drink and a revitalizing shower. Animals are everywhere in our world, and we should all do our part to shelter and preserve every species, so that we may enjoy them, while also allowing each species to thrive and flourish successfully and continuously.

18 CONSONANT SOUNDS

SUMMER MAGIC

Consonant /m/ sound as in map

That misty Monday morning, Maria awoke to the musical sounds of mimicking mockingbirds outside her bedroom window. She rose and dressed immediately, musing about the program for the marvelous day ahead. Maria had plans with her friends Thomas, Gemma and Matt to go out on Matt's motorboat. She hadn't met up with them since the previous autumn and was very eager to see them again. Matt had heard rumors of a mysterious cove only accessible by boat. After meeting at Maria's home at 9am, the four of them ambled down the marshy path that led to the community marina. The golden phragmites swayed calmly in the breeze to the music of the wind. The summer sun had broken through the mist, making the water shimmer like dancing diamonds. The friends climbed into the motorboat and Matt nimbly moved the boat off the ramp into the murky water. All were smiling and laughing as they zoomed away to embark on their mission.

Twenty minutes later, Matt raised the palm of his hand and motioned towards a slight half-moon bend in the shoreline. He aimed the motorboat in that direction and maneuvered it into the most magnificent tiny cove that they had ever seen. The four friends clambered out of the boat and took in the marvelous view. Golden sandbars surrounded them, with a small stream cutting across the middle of the most massive one. Clams, mussels and other mollusks were jumbled all over the beach. Seagulls screamed overhead, as miniscule piping plovers romped at the margin of the surf. It was truly a magical place and it was all theirs for that summer morning. After spending many hours meandering along the sandbars and examining the cove, Matt, Maria, Gemma and Thomas had to make their way back home. Tired, but so animated, they motored back smoothly and comfortably, dreaming of the next time they would visit their mysterious, magical cove of enchantment.

18 CONSONANT SOUNDS
THE BIRD'S NEST

Consonant /n/ sound as in nest

Nori and Ned were newlyweds looking for the perfect new home. They were meeting with their realtor, Tanner Randall, at nine o'clock that chilly spring morning to look at three different houses. The first house was a large colonial, far above their budget, but very convenient to town. Nori and Ned liked the lines of the house, but knew the payments would drain their budget. So onward they went to the next house.

The second house was a charming cottage on the outskirts of town. It was old and needed much work, but was affordable. Behind the cottage was a small pond–nice to look at but swarming with gnats and mosquitoes. It also had an antiquated heating system that didn't keep the house warm enough in winter. Nori whispered to Ned that they would both get pneumonia there if it wasn't updated, which would be an enormous expense. Onward they all went to house number three.

The third house was a newer ranch on a quiet lane that was not as close to town as the other two homes. As Nori, Ned and Tanner went up the steps to the front porch, Nori heard a funny sound coming from the lone flowerpot sitting there. As she gently pushed aside the branches of the plant, Nori began to kneel down and saw a gray and brown mourning dove sitting calmly on a nest of several eggs. "Oh", said Nori, "These are my very favorite birds—so gentle and calm, singing their mournful songs each morning. I know this must be a sign of luck about this house," she whispered to Ned. Sure enough, the ranch house turned out to be the best house they had seen, and was well within their budget. Their offer on the ranch was soon accepted, and Nori and Ned moved into their new home within weeks. Soon after, the sounds of the newly hatched baby mourning doves filled the air, and the couple knew that the luck of the bird's nest had helped them find their dream home.

18 CONSONANT SOUNDS
PICKING THE PERFECT PET

Consonant /p/ sound as in pig

Owning a pet can be a rewarding experience for plenty of people. Pets bring purpose, companionship, happiness and also responsibility into our lives. It's optimal to spend plentiful time to research specific animals in order to determine which pet will be perfect for you.

Cats and dogs are probably the most popular pets chosen by the population. Research has proven that both animals help to ease stress and lower blood pressure. Cats, kittens, puppies and dogs can be either adopted or purchased. Do ample research to plan which breed or type will appeal to you most and best complement your lifestyle and personality. You can do your research by computer, telephone or through books and photographs. Pay attention to your capital budget as well–purchasing and possessing a pet can be an expensive proposition!

Apart from cats and dogs, there are plenty of other types of pets that can be pleasing. A good starter pet is a betta fish or a gold fish, both of which require the least possible care and can be used to prepare even young people for responsibility. Particular reptiles such as snakes and iguanas are popular pets as well. Some people even own pot-bellied pigs as pets, as they are unexpected and peculiar. The plentiful varieties of birds prove to be phenomenal pets as well. From chirping canaries, to perky parakeets, to expressive parrots and even to proud peacocks with their pretty plumage, the options for pet bird choices are expansive. No matter which pet you prefer, just make sure you pick the one perfect for your personality and lifestyle. Pets can add ample happiness, pleasure and appreciation to our lives.

18 CONSONANT SOUNDS
THE SURPRISE

Consonant /r/ sound as in rat

Margery's alarm rang at 6:30, bright and early one frosty winter morning on January 10th. She rose rapidly and quietly to get ready, so as not to rouse her husband Herbert and their son Barry. She was traveling to the large department store Macy's, to perform inventory. Inventory meant enumerating all the merchandise is the Housewares Department, where she worked at a part-time job. Inventory was done once in the winter and then repeated again in the summer. Unfortunately, the winter inventory was generally done on January 10th, which was Margery's birthday. Not a great way to celebrate, she grumbled to herself.

Once inventory was over for the day, Margery wearily drove home. She was grimy, dirty, tired and cranky, and just wanted a shower and rest. Herbert and Barry greeted her at the door and hollered, "Hurry up–no time for a shower–we're going to a restaurant straightaway!" "What?!" protested Margery. "I have no desire to go out–I really want to remain at home and just relax!" With considerable persuasion, she grudgingly got into the car, and continued to grumble and wring her hands during the entire ride. Even the rhythmic drone of the car motor was not enough to comfort her. Having had enough of the grousing, Barry finally said, "Mom, this is terribly wrong. Please don't repeat this at my wedding!" With that, they all had to grin.

The three of them finally arrived at one of their favorite Chinese restaurants, where Margery discovered her family and many friends gathered around a large table. "Surprise!" they all cheered. The room was brimming with perfectly wrapped presents and fragrant flowers. The partygoers had driven from near and far to help Margery celebrate her red-letter day. What had started out as a dreary birthday turned into a most wonderful and memorable celebration that she rhapsodized over for the entire next year!

18 CONSONANT SOUNDS

HOW TO USE THE NEW YORK CITY SUBWAY SYSTEM

Consonant /s/ sound as in sun

One of the best and most efficient ways to get around New York City (NYC) is by using the extensive subway system. The subway system can get you to almost any location in NYC, and has come a long way since the days of the horse and buggy. There is even a direct stop right at the Museum of Natural History, where you can see many wonders of science and our natural world. Here are some steps to help make your subway travel easier.

1. Whether you are a tourist or a resident, first get yourself a city map and a subway map. The city map will show you a

list of locations of subway stations but not the entire system. For more detailed instructions, get yourself a subway map. These maps will help you plan out your trip before you go, both destination and timewise. Ask a nice station agent for a free subway map.

2. Purchase a refillable MetroCard through a subway station MC Vending Machine. They can also be purchased at other locations, including ticket machines at Long Island Railroad (LIRR) stations. The current fare, as of April 2016, is $2.75 per ride, when using a Pay-Per-Ride MetroCard. Additional amounts on MetroCards are available also. Check online or with a ticket agent at the station for other options. Transfers are also available and can be used on the subway and on NYC buses.

3. Once you have your MetroCard, locate and head toward the platform where your train will stop. Find a turnstile near the platform entrance and swipe your card with the MC name facing toward you quickly, in one smooth move. When the turnstile screen says "Go", walk through the turnstile speedily. Then proceed to the platform. Assess the overhead platform signs and stand near the correct sign indicating your

destination. Don't stand too close to the tracks for safety reasons–the trains speed by with the force of a cyclone! It can be very crowded and busy at times and seem like a circus, but following these suggestions will assure your safety.

4. Once the train approaches, look at the front of the train to make sure it is the one you want. The trains are labeled with numbers, letters and sometimes colors, so be aware of which train you need to board. Wait for the train to come to a complete stop once it arrives and allow the onboard passengers to egress before you board. Sit in the first seat you see, if any are available. If you must stand, be sure to hold tightly and securely to a pole or overhead bar. The train may make sudden starts and stops!

5. Although most New Yorkers are courteous and helpful if you need to ask a question, it's best to use good psychology and avoid making unnecessary eye contact or engaging in conversations with strangers. It just isn't considered appropriate.

6. Be aware of the stops your train is making by observing the signs on the walls as you pass each stop. It is often difficult

to hear the audio instructions, but still try to listen carefully to the announcements. Once you have reached your correct stop, wait for the train to come to a complete standstill and exit carefully. Watch the gap! Find the staircase that leads up to the street and enjoy your adventure in NYC!

18 CONSONANT SOUNDS
TIM'S TINY TURTLE

Consonant /t/ sound as in top

Tim Tuttle was a first grader at the Tremont Elementary School. He liked his teacher, Mr. Thomas, who was patient, smart, and very understanding. Tim also had many friends in his class, including Tyler, Betty, Tony and Tamara. One Tuesday morning, all four of his friends rushed into the classroom to tell Tim that a new pet store had just opened in town and they had all gotten turtles as pets. Tim was very excited and wanted a turtle, too. He decided he would ask his mother to bring him to the pet store after school so that he could get a turtle, as well.

After school, Mrs. Tuttle brought Tim to the pet store to look at the turtles. Unfortunately, they only had one left and it was a very tiny turtle. Tim held back bitter tears because it was so small, but his mother assured him that good things come in small packages and he should get that turtle, no matter that it was small. So Tim took his new pet home and promptly named him Tiny.

When Mr. Thomas heard that several of his students had turtles as pets, he got the brilliant idea to have a turtle race in the classroom. All the students were very excited! Mr. Thomas ripped up a big sheet of cardboard with sides around it so that the turtles would stay in that area. The turtle race was to be the next morning. Tim was very worried that Tiny would lose because of his small size, but again his mother told him not to worry. The next morning, the turtles were all placed on the starting line, being held in place by their owners. On the count of three, the students took their hands away and off went the turtles. Tony's turtle was ahead at first, but then he tripped and fell behind. Betty's turtle was now in first place, but suddenly little Tiny got a burst of speed and took the lead. Tim was cheering him on as Tiny crossed the finish line first. He picked up his little Tiny, gently tapped and petted his shell, and told Tiny that he couldn't have done any better!

18 CONSONANT SOUNDS

AVALON

Consonant /v/ sound as in van

Nestled in the quiet village of Stony Brook, NY, lies the very beautiful Avalon Park and Preserve. Avalon is a privately owned nature preserve spread out across nearly 70 acres of attractive woodlands. It is free to visitors and is open from dusk to dawn. The preserve was created by the Paul Simons Foundation to honor the memory of Paul Simons, an avid sportsman who enjoyed many outdoor activities. His family hopes that his vibrant and creative energy will be remain alive in the spirit of the preserve.

Avalon invites visitors to view five distinct natural habitats covered by native plants and trees. Trail maps are available at the entrance to Avalon to guide visitors through the various creatively designed divisions of the preserve. Tranquil ponds alive with ducks, geese and swans provide vibrant songs that would make Stephen Foster proud. Brave velvety-black cormorants arrive in the spring and entertain visitors by diving into the murky water to retrieve live fish. Leaving the pavement, visitors walk along wooden avenues that wind through verdant plantings of native trees and plants. Wildflower fields thrive throughout the spring and summer, covered with clover, violets and a variety of many other lovely flowers. Vines and shrubs mark the pathways through the woodlands vicinities, and the brave of heart can make the climb up to the contemplative labyrinth area. Once there, observe the heavenly view and clear your mind of all vexation. For a day of tranquility, relaxation and an unbelievable connection to nature, you've got to visit the preserve that is Avalon.

18 CONSONANT SOUNDS

WINTER WONDERLAND

Consonant /w/ sound as in wig

Winter–for workers commuting to work every day, winter can be challenging. Driving in snow and ice, bitter cold winds, and weary commuters dealing with public transit delays can make the season worrisome. Shoveling driveways and walkways, and cleaning off vehicles can become tiresome as well.

But...

If we look beyond the negatives of winter weather, we can enjoy the unique wonder of the season, such as...

- Waking up early and looking out your window at the brilliant blanket of white that has covered your lawn;

- Hearing the wild whoops of joyful children throwing snowballs at each other because they have a snow day;

- Seeing the scarlet red wings of a cardinal sitting watchfully on a snow-covered telephone wire;

- Putting on warm woolen socks and gloves that you haven't worn since last winter to go walk in the snow;

- Watching a choir walk from house to house to sing holiday carols;

- Quickly sticking out your warm tongue to catch a few wet snowflakes falling from the sky;

- Taking an evening stroll through wild white woods and whistling back to a wise old owl perched on a willow branch–whoo, whoo, whoo!;

- Watching the wind blow the light snow gently around into swirling twisters in the air;

- Blowing soft, powdery snow off the tops of wilted flower heads;

- Contemplating the view of lacy snow twirled around woody tree trunks and wiry branches;

- Marveling at wondrous icicles as long as your arm seeming welded to roofs and ledges.

Why not enjoy the wonders of the winter season and take the inconveniences in stride? For without winter, we would not be able to welcome the wonderment of the coming spring!

18 CONSONANT SOUNDS

YES OR NO

Cononant /y/ sound as in yell

Tanya and Yanni met at a wedding one year earlier. Tanya was the younger sister of the bride, Yolanda, and Yanni was the younger brother of the groom, Yogi. They had never seen each other before, yet developed an instant bond during that event. They became inseparable after that and discovered they had many common interests. Both Tanya and Yanni had graduated from Yale University and both lived in New York City. Yoga, yo-yo twirling, traveling to exotic places like Yemen and Guyana, and watching old movies while gobbling up pizza with onions were some of their favorite things to do. Both Tanya and Yanni had been yearning for that special someone and were elated to have found that in each other.

After about one year of dating, Yanni decided to ask Tanya to marry him. He was fairly sure she would say yes, but what if she said no?! Yanni planned out the perfect proposal, starting off with finding just the right engagement ring. He visited several jewelry stores in his area, but nothing caught his eye. Yanni decided to go yonder towards the neighborhood of his youth, and found a shop that had the exact ring he had been imagining. Hallelujah, yippee, yeah! The shop owner shared his opinion and Yanni purchased the ring. Before returning home, he bought a huge bouquet of yellow yarrow, Tanya's favorite flower, as well as some onions, tomato sauce and yeast to make their special pizza. Once home, Yanni placed the flowers into a vase and tied the ring onto one of the yarrow stems with yellow yarn, making sure it faced his seat and not Tanya's. Tanya soon arrived home, yawning after a long day at work as a youth counselor, and said she wanted to eat and then get to bed early. After they had finished their delicious dinner, Yanni turned the vase around so that Tanya could clearly see the ring. She was speechless. Yanni got down on one knee and asked Tanya to marry him. After what seemed like an eternity, Tanya smiled at Yanni and with tears in her eyes said … yes!!!

18 — CONSONANT SOUNDS

SUNRISE AT THE ZOO

Consonant /z/ sound as in zip

Hazy sunlight streamed in zigzags across the bars of the mighty gorillas' nighttime enclosure. They stretched and yawned, knowing that soon breakfast would be served. They lazily ambled outside for a day in the breezy fresh air and guzzled down their fruit and water, provided by their handler Zeke. If they lived in an actual jungle, perhaps in Tanzania or Zanzibar, instead of the zoo, Zeke sometimes fantasized that his gorillas might be friends with the fictional character *Tarzan*. *Tarzan* was the subject of many of author Edgar Rice Burroughs' famous stories. Swinging from vines and zooming from tree to tree, perhaps his gorillas would have amazing adventures every day!

In another zone of the zoo, three striped zebras were zooming out of their enclosure, waiting for their handler, Lizzy, to groom them before breakfast. Lizzy used a sharp pair of scissors to trim the bristly manes of the zebras, who were named Ozzy, Ziggy and Zelda. Once the grooming was finished, they resumed zipping around their maze-like enclosure, stopping only to graze on the tender grass and to swat away the flies that buzzed around them.

As the sun rose high in the sky, all of the zoo animals woke from their snoozing, and were prepared for another day of zealous children and observant adults. Birds were calling like melodious xylophones, elephants were trumpeting as they were sprayed on their noses by water hoses, and crazy monkeys were teasing each other while swinging from the trees. As anyone who has ever visited a zoo knows, spending a day with animals of all shapes and sizes is a very pleasing way to spend a day!

7 DIAGRAPHS

LUCKY CHARM

Digraph /ch/ sound as in chin

Charlie was charging down the crowded stretch of the busy street one chilly morning, hoping he would be able to catch the bus to make it to work on time. He made the bus just in time, and by chance, just before boarding, he spied a dime on the ground. Charlie picked it up and chucked it into the chest pocket of his trench coat. The bus was very crowded and he began to search for a seat. Luck was with him and Charlie snatched an empty chair. He made it to work on time and got to action on the batch of papers he had left on the bench in his office.

Charlie worked quickly and before long a bunch of his friends came to question him as to whether he was ready for lunch.

He was so busy working, he wasn't watching the clock for the time. He stretched his legs and cheerfully went to lunch with his chums. They went to a nearby Chinese restaurant, and Charlie hoped they would still have some of his favorite dish, chicken with chestnuts, cheese and peaches. Lucky again–he managed to get the last serving, and they even made it for him without any cheese! Charlie was so cheerful that he treated all his chums to lunch using his chip credit card.

Back at work, Chance, who was in charge of Charlie's department, called Charlie into his office. Chance informed him that Charlie had been chosen to be the chief of a new branch of the office, which also meant a big raise in pay. Lucky again! As he happily made his way home, Charlie checked the chest pocket of his trench coat again, and touched the dime he had found that morning. What a righteous good luck charm that dime was, he chuckled to himself. From now on, he would continue to look for more lucky charm dimes in the future!

7 DIAGRAPHS

SHARKS

Digraph /sh/ sound as in ship

Sheila was very excited to hear that her cousin Shawn was coming to visit her for a short vacation in Shinnecock, Long Island, NY. Shawn lived in Washington State and had never seen the Atlantic Ocean. Shawn was excited to be making the trip and was looking forward to seeing some sharks in the waters around Shinnecock. He was an avid shark enthusiast and knew a lot about the various species of the great fish. Shawn was looking forward to sharing his knowledge of sharks with Sheila.

When Shawn arrived in NY, he took the train from the airport to Shinnecock, where Sheila met him at a nearby station. They got settled in Sheila's beach shanty and had a cool drink in the shade outside. "What do you want to do first?" asked Sheila. Shawn shouted that he wanted to go to the beach right away, so off they went. As they approached the water, Shawn could hear the crash of the waves and the smell of the salty air. He asked Sheila if there were many varieties of sharks in that area, but she replied that she wasn't sure. She knew there were small sand sharks near shore, but felt that the larger types, even Great White Sharks, were further out in the ocean, and would require a special trip out on a fishing boat, further from the shore. They made a plan to take that boat trip the next day.

As they boarded the fishing boat the following morning and left the shallow waters, Shawn could hear the crash of the waves against the boat and felt the shock of the engines as the machines picked up speed. He felt some tension, but his excitement soon took over. Shawn knew some people hunted sharks for sport, but his conscience told him it was wrong. After being patient for a long while, they spotted the fin of a large shark flashing through the ocean. Then the shark leapt into the air, causing a great splash. Shawn could barely contain his excitement! Both Shawn and Sheila agreed it was a very special day and knew it was a memory that would last a lifetime!

7 DIAGRAPHS

SOUTH TO PORTSMOUTH

Unvoiced /th/ sound as in thongs

Voiced /th/ sound as in feather

It was finally summertime and the Smith family of Bath, England, was excitingly planning where they would go for their annual vacation. Their big decision was whether to travel north or south. Their home in Bath is a famous tourist destination, located in the rolling countryside of southwest England. Bath is known for its natural hot springs, 18th century architecture, and for the renowned Roman-built baths and wonderful museums. Bath actually became a UNESCO World Heritage Site in 1987, and is a thoroughly wonderful place to live and visit.

After doing some online research, Father thought going south to Portsmouth would be the best choice. Portsmouth, on England's south coast, was only about a 2 hour drive from Bath and had many interesting attractions they would all enjoy. Portsmouth is a port city and naval base, and is known for its maritime heritage. It is the U.K's only island city, located mainly on Portsea Island. Like Bath, Portsmouth's history can be traced back to Roman times. Thea and Theo, the thirteen year old twins, were both thrilled that there was also the Blue Reef Aquarium, which was known for its underwater viewing tunnel. Mother was interested in learning more about Portsmouth's famed residents, which included some of her favorite authors such as Charles Dickens, Rudyard Kipling and H.G. Wells. Father was eager to visit the Portsmouth Historic Dockyard, the D-Day Museum, and the Mary Rose, a raised Tudor shipwreck. There was something for everyone in Portsmouth!

The Smith family was thrilled with the decision to vacation in Portsmouth that summer. They got about to packing, as they would be leaving early Thursday morning, which was only three days away. Thea packed her new leather thongs as her footwear, and Theo was going to wear his new hat with the thrush feather on it. This would be a thoughtful and memorable adventure for them all!

7 DIAGRAPHS

"WH" QUESTIONS AND MORE!

Digraph /hw/ sound as in whip

"Wh" words are very important in English, as they are used in many types of questions.

Who/whom are used for questions about people. Who has arrived at the door? Tom is at the door. Who wants pizza? We all want pizza! Who is she sitting next to? She is sitting next to Ms. Whitman.

What is used for questions about somebody or something. What is this? This is a battery charger. What did he say to do? He said to sit down. What did they do? They went to the store.

When is used to get information about a time period in which something happened, or will happen. When will he arrive? He will arrive at 6pm. When can we meet? I'm not free until Saturday. When was the show? The show was last night.

Where is used to get information on a location. Where do you live? I live in New York City. Where were the car keys? The keys were on the table. Where did you go yesterday. I went to the beach.

Why is used to get information on the reason something happened. Why is the house locked? Because no one is home. Why didn't John stay? Because he had to go to work. Why didn't you call me? I didn't call because my cell wasn't charged.

Which is used to get information on a comparison between two or more similar things. Which headphones do you prefer? I prefer the cheaper ones. Which river is the longest? I think it is the Nile. Which subway line would be faster? The "A", because it's an express train.

Whose is used to get information on who owns something. Whose knapsack is this? It's mine. Whose idea was it? It was Frank's idea. Whose puppy is that playing over there? I don't know.

7 DIAGRAPHS

Don't confuse "whose" and "who's"! Who's is the contraction of who is. They are both pronounced the same, however.

The following is a short story using "wh" words:

Whitey always wanted to be a cowboy, as he loved horses and being outdoors. Every chance he got, he would go to the stables to help take care of the horses. Whitey was lucky, as his best friend Jeff's father owned the stables. "What can I do today?", he'd ask everytime he arrived. Jeff's dad, Mr. Whitman would always whistle while he thought about what Whitey could do. Usually, it would be to brush, feed, or walk the horses. Whitey loved it all.

The only problem was that everytime Whitey was around the stables, he would start to sneeze. Oh, great, he thought. I love horses, but I'm allergic to them! One day, while feeding the horses their oats (their staple food), Whitey had a particularly bad allergic reaction Whitey worried that he'd have to stop going to the stables. However, Mr. Whitman, who was working nearby, called Whitey to follow him to the chicken coop next to the horse barn. Whitey started sneezing uncontrollably! Mr.

Whitman aaid, "Whitey, you're not allergic to horses, but you are to chickens!" Or you might be allergic to the wheat that we feed the chickens. From now on, when you work with the horses, take them over to the other side of the farm, which is away from the chicken coops. I bet that will stop the sneszing."

As it turned out, that was not just a whim. Mr. Whitman was right, Whitey was indeed allergic to the chickens. His father took him to an allergist, who said he was allergic to birds and fowl. From then on, Whitey never again went near the chickens while helping it at the stables.

7 DIAGRAPHS
SING

Digraph /ng/ sound as in wing

MORNING

Ingrid's alarm began ringing at 6 am that spring morning. Her favorite artist was singing her favorite song as the alarm rang. Music—the best way to wake up in the morning, Ingrid thought! She went to the sink to brush her teeth and then turned on the shower. As she showered, Ingrid continued singing the song she had awoken to. She sang at the top of her lungs, the words just rolling off her tongue. After dressing and eating a quick breakfast, Ingrid was out the door and off to her teaching job.

AFTERNOON

Ah, finally lunch time. Ingrid's Kindergarten class had gone along with her teacher's aide to the cafeteria, where they were all singing the tune they were learning in music class. Ingrid and her gang of friends were sitting outside in the warm sunshine, eating and chatting. Bees were buzzing their busy songs amongst the pink flowers near the picnic tables. Sterling was reading a very long book about King Arthur and hoping that none of the bees would sting him. Ingrid and Inga were enjoying the warm spring sun, while telling each other what things had gone wrong that morning. Laughing, they both then broke into a funny song about having a bad day and instantly felt better. No longer angry, they went back to class when the bell rang and had the strength to have a more pleasant afternoon.

EVENING

With her workday over, Ingrid was driving back home, cheerfully singing along to the car radio. She happily prepared a light dinner and sat outside to eat. Ingrid could hear the songs of the frogs croaking in her pond and of the owls hooting in the nearby woods. She smiled and began singing a childhood lullaby softly to herself. No matter how bad the day, how unpleasant the weather, or how down she felt, Ingrid knew that all she had to do to make herself feel better was to…sing!

7 DIAGRAPHS

TRIP TO THE BANK

Digraph /nk/ as in sink

Frank's Uncle Hank asked him to go to the bank, as he was not feeling well. He told Frank exactly what to do, as Uncle Hank was very organized and liked things done his way. Frank was happy to be able to help his favorite uncle.

On the way to the bank, Frank (as usual) started to daydream and soon realized his mind was a complete blank regarding his errand. As always, whenever Frank became nervous he would begin to blink his eyes uncontrollably. This really stinks, he thought to himself. Wow! What should I do now? Just as he was on the brink of panic, he decided to force himself to remain calm and have something cold to drink. As he drank the pink lemonade from his backpack, he tried to recall exactly what Uncle Hank had asked him to do. He remembered the money and slips of paper his uncle had given him, so he thrust his hand into his pocket and yanked out a hunk of cash, coins, and some pieces of paper. With that, Frank heard the clink of change hitting the sidewalk and saw a quarter roll into the gutter. As he stepped off the sidewalk to retrieve the quarter, a car honked for him to get out of the street. The car passed, Frank looked both ways, and he picked up the quarter. He then calmly counted the money and realized he was ten dollars short. His heart sank. He knew his uncle wouldn't spank him, but he felt very sad, nonetheless.

Frank arrived at the bank, and did everything his uncle had asked. He plunked the cash, change, and slips of papers into the teller's tray and paid attention to make sure everything was done the way Uncle Hank had asked. Frank then started for home. All the way, he kept thinking about the lost ten dollars and what he would say to his uncle. Frank was in a real funk.

Once he had arrived home, his Uncle Hank rushed to the door and said, "Frank, I'm so sorry! I made an error and gave you ten dollars too little. I hope you didn't think you had lost it!" Frank was happy to hear the news that he hadn't lost the money and didn't disappoint his uncle. He thanked his uncle, feeling really good that he was off the hook. His uncle said, "Because I made the mistake, I want you to have the ten dollars that I forgot to give you. Go and buy yourself something!"

Frank thanked his Uncle Hank again, and ran out to meet his friends. They would go out for an ice cream and get their favorite sundaes with the 'tip' that his uncle had generously given to him. Frank was surely out of his funk!

CONTROLLED VOWELS

THE CIRCUS GIRL

Controlled vowel /ur/ as in bird & hurt

Practically since birth, my cousin Pearl wanted to be in the circus. Whenever the circus came to town, she yearned to go. She begged her sister to help convince their mother to take them. At first my aunt would spurn the idea, but when Pearl would purr like a kitten, my aunt would relent and take them. Pearl would rush to get ready and almost flew like a bird out of the house in excitement. My aunt just rolled her eyes and hoped that Pearl would grow out of the "circus stage" and dream about a different career to pursue.

My uncle, Pearl's father, was a preacher and my aunt was a nurse. Both of her parents hoped that Pearl would choose a career that was more stable than life in the circus. Maybe a teacher, lawyer, or nurse like her mother. But she remained true to her goal of being in the circus. For her parents, this felt like a curse.

Even though Pearl had been to the circus many times in the past, she would act surprised by the magician's tricks, even though she could probably perform those tricks herself! She would laugh hysterically at the clown, even when the jokes were not that funny and everyone else would just groan. Pearl was plain happy to be there, as the circus was really her happy place. She dreamed of the day when she would work there. That is how she got the nickname "Circus Girl".

When the rest of the family was really hungry or thirsty, Pearl wouldn't rush to go to the hamburger stand. She did not want anything to eat or drink, but wanted to continue to enjoy the circus.

The best part of the day for Pearl was the trapeze, which is what she wanted to do when she was a grown-up. She loved when the trapeze artists would fly high in the air, walk the tight rope, jump down, and land lightly on their feet.

CONTROLLED VOWELS

Finally, when it was time to leave the circus, Pearl would burn at the idea of not being able to stay longer. But everyone had to get up early the next day to go to church. The family of the preacher could never miss church! So Pearl had to come back down to earth and obey her parents. She left the circus dreaming about the next time the the circus would come to town.

CONTROLLED VOWELS

GOING FAR IN A CAR

Controlled vowel /ar/ as in park

Americans are very fond of their cars. There are approximately 276 million cars on American roads, which is about 3/4 of a car per person! There is nothing like taking a long car trip on a beautiful day out in the country. There is much to see in the rural parts of America. They, of course, are very different than what you see walking around any of the many congested American cities. In the country you are likely to see farms, barns, trees galore (with beautiful bark!), corn on the cob, and other fruits and vegetables growing everywhere. Many farms have stands out front, where you can buy their fresh crops, usually at bargain prices compared with stores in the cities.

You will also surely pass small towns with cute houses and lovely gardens to look at. Some places in the country have beautiful lakes, streams, and rivers where you might go fishing. Who knows? If you pack your fishing rod, you may catch a carp, cod, or bass. Might make for a delicious fish dinner!

You need to plan well before you take a long car trip. You must make sure you have enough gas in the tank, water in the radiator, and air in the tires. It is also a good idea to pack some snacks and drinks, especially water. A little dark chocolate would be great, too! Even though most smart phones have excellent navigation systems, it is fun to bring an old fashioned paper map, which shows attractions that may be close-by. If you bring a picnic lunch, you're sure to find the perfect place under the shade of a very old tree.

The charm of the country can really be discovered best when going by car. You can see much more this way than if you travel by train or bus, where you only see trees, or highways. Trains and buses usually don't allow you to see the many beautiful small cities, towns, and villages.

CONTROLLED VOWELS

So the next time you have a day off, take a road trip and you I'll be amazed by what you will see and experience. It's really fun to go far in a car!

CONTROLLED VOWELS

THE SHORT STORM

Controlled vowel /or/ as in fork

The whole family was sitting on the large back porch of our home in Fort Lauderdale. I was born there and it was the only home I knew. At that time, Fort Lauderdale was a sleepy town twenty-eight miles north of Miami, nothing like the busy, large city that it is today. Now, there is a huge airport walking distance from the house and Port Everglades is also very close-by.

As is common in south Florida, rains come quickly in the summer and don't usually last very long. It may rain for fifteen or twenty minutes, but then the sun comes out as if nothing had happened. However, this one particular summer day, which was a real scorcher started out clear and calm. However, suddenly a storm formed and torrential rain started coming down in buckets. It was almost as if the sky were a huge bottle that someone had uncorked and a tremendous amount of water fell to earth. As the storm worsened, the wind kicked in and a giant gust ripped the roof off of our back porch. Luckily, we had all been escorted into the house by my father, who knew this wasn't a regular storm. This would be record breaker. Interestingly, the forecast had not predicted anything out of the ordinary for that day. The force of the water also cut a large gorge that ran alongside of our house and all the way down to the street. A small river of water cascaded into the road.

Regardless of how powerful the storm had been, it proved to be short, as is the usual pattern in south Florida. However, all of our corn in the large garden on the side of the house had been torn out of the ground by the strong winds. The short storm had done a great deal of damage, but luckily, the only thing destroyed on the house was the back porch roof. We temporarily patched it up with cardboard, and a few days later the workman came and put on a new roof, restoring it to its former condition.

CONTROLLED VOWELS

Days later, the mud had all been cleared from the streets, and the downed trees had all been chopped up and carted away. In fact, The hordes of workmen, who had arrived from many other states, were good sports and did an amazing job of getting Fort Lauderdale back in shape. Life went back to normal, but we often think about that short storm and how it had temporarily destroyed our house and yard. Now it's one of the many memories we have of our home.

3 DIPTHONGS

BOING, BOING, BOING

Dipthong /oi/ sound as in oil and boy

Very early one bright and breezy spring morning, Ribbitt the frog rubbed the winter from his sleepy eyes and decided to boldly venture outside. He observed that the snow had melted and in its place were buds of pale green beginning to burst into bloom on the pond plants. Ribbitt had slumbered for many months since the fall, as frogs hibernate to escape the bitter temperatures of winter. He had slowed his heartbeat and breathing, and lowered his body temperature to closely match the outside temperature. But now it was spring and time to venture out from the bottom of his beautiful blue pond!

Ribbitt felt the bright sun begin to warm his little green body. He bounced along the pebbles near the edge of the pond and thought he would go look for some of his buddies who lived nearby. He saw his friends Belle and Bobby, the bickering blue jays who lived behind the pond. Ribbitt waved hello and bounded off to look for his best buddy Robert, the box turtle, who lived near the bog. Robert, too, was awake and was slowly bobbing down the beach in a deliberate, determined manner. Boing, boing, boing–Ribbitt bounced quickly to meet up with Robert. When the two best buddies were beside each other, they both took a deep breath and basked in the incredible fresh air. Spring was back and so very enjoyable!

3 DIPTHONGS

OWL AT EVENING

Dipthong /ow/ sound as in ouch

Mr. Fowler wiped his brow with a towel and began dragging his plow toward the barn. He was a farmer and put in about 12 hours each day in the fields and tending to his animals. Mr. Fowler had several cows, some goats, and too many chickens to count. As he was making his way through the field down to the barn, he heard a strange sound coming from the woods. Could it be one of his many cats meowing while it chased a mouse? No, the sound seemed to come from above and not from the ground. He put the plow into the barn and went back outside to investigate.

As Mr. Fowler made his way south towards the woods, a light snow fell like powder all around him. Once again, he heard the same strange sound. Could it be one of his cows? No, he thought, they're all in the barn. He heard the howl of a dog in the distance, but knew that couldn't be the sound he had heard. All of a sudden the sound grew closer, and this time, Mr. Fowler looked up into the trees. There on a huge pine bough, sat a proud brown owl. Ah, thought Mr. Fowler, I have found the source of that strange sound. The owl looked at the farmer, opened his large mouth and hooted once again, before opening his powerful wings and flying off the bough. Mr. Fowler shouted goodbye to the owl and left the woods, bound for home. He was happy the mystery sound had been found and was ready for a relaxing evening at home now.

3 DIPTHONGS

LEARNING TO COOK

Dipthong /oo/ as in book and pull

It is surely a good thing for everyone to learn how to cook. Many years ago, only women were cooks and men would shy away from the kitchen. Things have changed and now many men can cook and some of the most famous cooks (and chefs!) in the world are men.

If someone wants to learn to cook, there are many cookbooks available for that purpose. These books list ingredients you will need and contain instructions on how much of each ingredient is necessary, how long something should be cooked and at what temperature. It isn't magic and, anyone who wants to, can learn to cook, even if they say, "Oh, I can't even boil water!"

Another way to learn to cook is to watch YouTube videos. Almost anything you can think of to cook has been posted as a video on YouTube. It would be a good idea to first watch the video all the way through and take notes about ingredients, amounts of each to use, time, temperature, etc. After you have assembled the ingredients, watch the video again while you cook, and pause the video as necessary.

Cooking is great for social gatherings, as many an enjoyable evening can be had over a home-cooked meal. However, before you cook something for friends, make sure you have already cooked and tasted it! If you like it, there's a much better chance that your friends will, too! It's a very bad idea to try out an untested recipe on guests!

Some helpful advice for being a good cook is to be very organized:

1. Keep your cooking utensils where they are easy to reach;

2. Put things back in the same place every time.

3. Pay close attention to the instructions given in the recipe.

4. Read recipes multiple times as you cook, so that you don't make mistakes.

Also, if you make any dish outside on the BBQ, make sure not to get any soot on the food. That would be yucky!

If you have any desire to learn to cook, you should do it. It can be a wonderful hobby, and if you're successful, it can be very delicious, too!

2 SPECIAL SOUNDS

NAUGHTY PAUL

Special sound /-aw/ as in jaw and haul

Of all my friends, Paul is the only one with the nickname "Naughty". It wasn't that he was a bad kid, but he was just... uh, naughty! He would go where he shouldn't go, do what he shouldn't do, and ALWAYS got caught! He wasn't good about getting away with things like other naughty kids were. His parents, teachers and friends always found out about his mischief and Paul was forever getting into trouble.q

Even though his parents tried to get him to talk softly in public places, he would always use a loud voice and someone would tell him to be quiet. Of course, he balked at this because he really liked to talk!

One time, on a school field trip to a musem, Paul crawled under a display case in order to hide and scare his classmates, but he triggered the alarm. Of course, Paul got caught and spent the rest of the day in the office of the museum director, who was not happy.

One day when his mother was doing the laundry, she noticed that Paul had drawn pictures all over his brand new T-shirt. She wasn't happy with Paul when the pictures did not come out in the wash, as he had used a permanent marker! His 'pictures' were really just ugly doodles, and the new shirt became a dusting cloth.

Paul's father also got angry with Paul the day he took us to a nearby lake in order for us to launch our new model boats. Everything was going smoothly until Paul got the not so bright idea to light a firecracker and put it in his boat. Well, because the firecracker had a long fuse, it didn't go off until the boat was 30-40 feet out in the lake. All of a sudden, the firecracker exploded and made a hole in the bottom of Paul's new, remote control boat. It slowly sank to the bottom of the lake while we helplessly watched. Paul's father had steam coming out of his ears!

2 SPECIAL SOUNDS

The dinner table was another place that Paul would act naughty. When his mother served him his dinner he would claw at his food like an animal and gnaw the meat like a tiger. Although he was just trying to be funny, no one was laughing.

Well, it's been a long time since those days when Paul was naughty, and Paul is all grown up and is now a lawyer. Even though he no longer does any of those things, his friends still call him by his nickname...Naughty Paul.

2 SPECIAL SOUNDS

A TRIP TO ASIA

Special sound /zh/ as in television

When the wonderful news came to Brigitte and Jacques of Baton Rouge, Louisiana, that their second granddaughter, Anastasia, had just been born, they were overcome with explosions of joy. They quickly made revisions to their usual travel plans and booked a trip to Asia. Anastasia had been born in Da Nang, Vietnam. Da Nang is a coastal city in central Vietnam on the South China Sea. The area is famous for its azure water beaches, the Marble Mountains and many beautiful Buddhist shrines. Vietnam is an interesting and most pleasurable place to visit and/or live in. Jacques and Brigitte made the decision to leave as soon as their visas were processed. They packed some casual and dressy clothes, as well as many presents for the baby.

Their family and friends wished them a bon voyage and off they flew to Asia.

The trip was a very long one, with a lay-over in Seoul, Korea, plus another flight to Da Nang. Despite the lengthy journey and airport confusion, the new grandparents spent their time trying to visualize how their new grandchild would look. Although Brigitte and Jacques were Caucasian and Anastasia was Asian, it made no difference to them. She would be their little treasure!

When the couple finally arrived at the Da Nang Airport, they were met by their son and an entourage of other family and friends. What a welcome! They drove to the large family home in a beige van and entered through a large garage door. Waiting at the rouge colored entrance for them was their daughter-in-law holding tiny Anastasia. Brigitte and Jacques nearly had a collision with each other trying to hold the baby first! Cradling precious Anastasia in her arms, Grandma Brigitte kissed her soft black hair and looked into her bright dark eyes. "Anastasia is such a long name for such a tiny girl. I will call you Zsa Zsa," declared Brigitte. It was a memorable and joyful occasion for them all!

www.ingramcontent.com/pod-product-compliance
Lightning Source LLC
Chambersburg PA
CBHW080940040426
42444CB00015B/3382